A Clearing

LOUISE CARSON

George Payerle, Editor

Signature EDITIONS

Cover design by Doowah Design.

Acknowledgements
Thanks to editors Allan Briesmaster and George Payerle, who, separately, advised me; and to all the poets who have critiqued my work.

Many of the poems in *A Clearing* were previously published in various books and chapbooks, including *Rope: A Tale Told in Prose and Verse, Mermaid Road, Twigs & Leaves,* Volumes 1,3,4 & 5, *Poets in the Griffintown Cultural Corridor,* Volume 2, and *Hang.* Some of were also published in the anthologies *Portrait of Greenwood, Passages: A Collection of Poems, Anthology of Montreal Writers,* and *29 words in solitude,* as well as the print and on-line magazines *Cahoots, Carousel, Contemporary Verse 2, The Dalhousie Review, Event, FreeFall, Jones Av., Montreal Serai, Other Voices, Sunday@6,* and *Vallum.*

This book was printed on Ancient Forest Friendly paper.
Printed and bound in Canada by Hignell Book Printing Inc.

We acknowledge the support of The Canada Council for the Arts and the Manitoba Arts Council for our publishing program.

Library and Archives Canada Cataloguing in Publication

Carson, Louise, 1957-, author

Poems.
ISBN 978-1-927426-63-0 (pbk.)

I. Title.

PS8605.A7775C43 2015 C811'.6 C2015-901414-X

Signature Editions
P.O. Box 206, RPO Corydon, Winnipeg, Manitoba, R3M 3S7
www.signature-editions.com

to friends

Contents

I

II

III

I

in a visual world

what can I do with words
that lie unnoticed
on the page

I can drape them with meat or
sit them in a bath of baked beans out on the street
every day for a month

I can wrap them around your island
red or pink to curve or droop
                                        flutter

we shall go and look down on them
cut or grown in a field
my meaningful shapes

they are words
they lie on the page
and hang in the air

Twice

A different fox but seen before too long ago
to be more or less than what it was as we
cross-country skied along railway tracks
no need for a moon, the snow made enough
light stolen from the day and the tracks straight
you know the way, you push ahead arms
pumping, breath timing the effort when
to the side visible parallel motion low
to the ground going as steadily its way as we
went ours, the we so soon to split apart. We paused.
It trotted on.

That in the car last night ascent of a
slight hill, attention focussed on my lights
and on the stripes laid down to keep me
straight eyes turned to the left
only this time the angle was convergent
and as I slowed and it broke stride
and turned back from the road I saw
the same fox, the red fur silvering,
watching me with the same eyes as before.
It paused. Was joy.
Was joy returned.

Muskrat dives

Muskrat dives, heavy, into a ditch.

  The water-sound shimmers like sheep bells.

(Yes, it's really like this where I live.)

  Today the light is yellow-orange and very clear.

Today I see a perfect yellow bird among the gray-brown crowd.

  If I were a hawk I'd dive at him: he'd taste so sweet.

The turtle

The turtle I passed four times today
caught in the deep grass at the side of the road
the fourth time put back in the muddy ditch
picked up by its shell, head drawing in and back claws dragging
at the skin of my wrists,
the turtle, for the first time,

flew   and I,

going past twice with a wolf on a string
twice jogging arms up, a small pale T. rex
an ancient bird twittering, offering compassion where none was
conceived
afraid of my suffering
last summer's jackrabbit's month-long decay and the smell
polluting my lyric way,

                              I flew   too.

I'm singing a song of daisies

I'm singing a song of daisies
in my head
toying with the phrases

camomile
late and lazy hybrid daisy
daisy days
in a daze
wild daisies
early
eager
first

when their music pierces my orbit
and all the words burst.

McDonald's, 32nd Avenue, Lachine

Now night, and off the curving yellow arches,
the light, usually so harsh, glows dull in summer's haze.
Moths leave it alone, cavort with brighter streetlights.

Cars move slowly, their noise softened.
Songs drift by — salsa, reggae — and quiet voices.
Even the motorcycles, summer's lords, are muffled.

Inside, under a strong white light, white women sit,
examine prospective customers. Outside,
a dusky terrace, where black kids lounge.

Across the street, people disappear down a dark lane
next to the used car lot: a scary little guy with two giggling girls,
a couple on a scooter, a man with a dog.

A fat old man wears a slender nasal lifeline with resignation.
Become a hybrid, battery and oxygen powered,
he parks his electric wheelchair near my car.

I turn the key to check the time and the headlights play
on the thighs, smooth and hairless, of a girl on rollerblades.
Passively she glides.

Her boyfriend on his bike smiles,
his arm around her waist, and tows her
back to their place.

It is a night (the critics might say) of lyric intensity —
applause that we come out and take our marks and with our flesh
make the scene:
that we are here, and here, there's ice cream.

Stream of Israel

It's the next year in Jerusalem.
We've agreed to meet —
you from Rumania, me from Canada —
a recovering Christian, a non-observing Jew.
Marriages, children aborted, we visit
both the burial places of Mary, wonder at her choices.
In a thin-sided, clanking little car
we take frozen water bottles and a few clothes
into the desert where anything can happen:
where a one-handed, born-again skydiver
might land and be known to us as Charlie:
where waiting to pick him up might be Captain Fuad,
late of the Lebanese army, working now as a journalist.
So when we settle for lunch on a remote dusty terrace
or rush to supper in a narrow café
the mix is vital: helicopter aerial photography,
fishing with dynamite, art and music desperate
for North American representation.
Driving to the coast we thumb our noses at Caesar,
at the Crusaders, their walls, aquaducts, arenas:
instead slide into a dark old town and a dirty sea.
A cold shower that night probably saves my life.
Up to Lebanon and back: border guards, kibbutzim, oranges,
a city on a mountain. At the top you offer me
exactly nothing but the view. I take it and I leave it,
keep three sandy potsherds picked from the rubble
of the walls of the City of David: one for Muslim,
one for Christian, one for Jew.

A clearing

It takes guts to go into the woods
when you're used to fields and orchards and lanes.
All that stuff about darkness — you fear.

But there's usually a clearing somewhere in there.
Man-made: buzz-cut or burnt, ploughed or trampled.
Or made by some giant toppling — and the land brambles over.

I know where there's a field of corn
enclosed on all sides by trees,
except where it opens for the farmer's tractor.
Old tracks, these.

Fence posts aslant, earth sprouting wire,
ghostly cow pastures, the odd mature maple,
where, a hundred years past,
the farmer ate his bread and cheese.

And older,
the narrow trails that follow the contour
around large rocks or watery low spots.
The dog sniffs them out and I see from a height
where others slipped through, carried babies or weapons,
moving soft on the mould, on the mould we make,
seeing trillums, say, white turning to pink,
and light, the same light, opening.

Where the old can sit, the children play,
where the wild fruit grows,
where we spread our clothing to dry.

Tulips

Smelling lilacs in the rain, we can't believe in winter.
Still cool but now, at least, wrapped in green, we can linger;
admire peas and lettuce and look for the carrot seeds' confirmation;
unkink our hunched cold necks, stretch and let it take us over;
squander our affection on a sweet-smelling, two-toned,
double-ruffled daffodil named Tahiti.

Now we will live in the weeks of tulips — pink, red, purple;
swirling, creamy, autonomous, cool-cupped breasts.
Nipple down, their green stems pull them to the ground.

Flirting with David

Huge magnolia buds before the trees leaf out:
your Carolinian forest opening.

Smaller fruit trees, screens of pink,
your wild cherries: Asian associations.

Far north and underneath,
my little blues tug at the ground: ephemeral.

I name them — scilla, chionodoxa — and your eyes warm.
Your pleasure is in the words.

Basal. Raceme. Toward the apex, and in succession,
an elongated axis bears flowers.

About the epicactus

Who knew that this irregular, no,
gangling frame, its intermittent arms
attenuations punctuated with hair,
and with no claim to beauty
save its dull green, its weird silhouette
doubled, dark against a yellow wall,
in form a thin vegetable scream,

had hid such a sun of a flower,
a blend of orange, white, gold and cream,
to blaze one day, one night, to a depth
of daring, glowing, open lust,
at which we stare, creation's door ajar.

And then the slow wilt, the drop, till ... ah ...
the green vein stops at a calloused scar.

petal

a dissolving
  in water   air

a fine thinness
  there

an inward slit-eyed glance
  a holy tongue of fire
    dance the soul up
      from root to sacred colour

a sprint with light in time

a petal
  then   another

between times

feast all day —
some can

I need
more contrast than —

for example

that, then
this, now

in between
is when

I sail the seas

sky in bird

after René Magritte's painting *la Grande Famille*

if sky in bird
then soil in man

peel back palm's skin

there
a pebble
a tiny curled shell
embedded in dirt

and the false mirror
(the artist's eye)
reflects the cloudy blue
on a bit of feathered earth

from a collection of feathers

Sun flickers on the wall as steam rises from tea.

  Birds flying across the sun leave quick shadows on the wall.

Sliced yellow fruit contains all the sweetness of this room,

  its bitter skin peeled away.

Birds drop like leaves from the tree.

  The wind shakes the tree for feathers.

I put one in my hat, where it disappears.

Waiting

Planting spring in autumn
as cool wet chlorophyll recedes,
as day length crisps each minute and hour,
and living things darken and thin.

Waiting for green to poke up
through rough earth, dead leaves;
hopeful seven months are enough
to pay for one month's beauty.

Trying to believe a spring follows this winter.
Struggling with the images
of what it might look like.
Imagining the flower.

The fields begin to sheathe themselves

The fields begin to sheathe themselves in some
soft metal underfoot as they ripen
into hardness. The air quiets. Except
for Christmas' three-week hum, traffic thins.
Some life has left the earth, been driven down
and in. The metal spreads its silent hymn
that sings of hardship, night; of frozen beings,
their signals lost; records the broken keen
of almost-dogs. They spread out as they run
for meat. Under the trees their lines bisect
the rabbits' shorter curves. Life joins life:
gray fur, brown fur, metallic scent of blood.

The economy 2011

Don't make the birds wait
for seed in this cold winter.
To the hardware store to buy it
though it's Christmas Eve.
To the little store to throw
a little money as though the owner
and his wife and child
are chickadees pecking in dry snow.

First Christmas, after

The mother dresses herself, puts down tea and book,
straps on the accoutrement of fidelity;
goes shopping. This for that one, that for this:
the gifts admit the pure impossibility
of future bliss. She seeks to cover
the minimum, based on expenditure,
that none can say, though they might suspect,
she's unmoved by the day.

And as she drives from store to store and drops
cash here, asks for credit there, she dreams
of what she knows she's moving toward:
a soft eve, the shops closed, the rushing traffic hushed.
At home, far from the tinsel and the glut,
a candle flickers for the things she's lost.

Fuel prices (for the Luddites)

Maybe not you but certainly I,
living freelance, untenured, unpartnered,

will be wrapped in layers of wool
found at church basement sales,

possibly will even wear the news
next to my skin,

will finally lose that last ten pounds
deciding a roof matters more

than a full stomach with scant privacy
out there.

Already I visit the woods after storms,
pick up dead wood for kindling,

shed the last two hundred years.

What is a country?

The stricken one turns on her side
asks what is that bird whose sweet song
wakes me the doctor leans close whispers
we all of us only guess at its name perhaps
the dying hear the soul singing what
is a bird without its feathers a country
without its young the boy's dead body
what's under the flag his father's face or
under that his hands release white flight
a box is built a post is sunk between's attached
a wire where the doves sit.

Enough

It will   kill me
I am   dying in
this heaviness   as new
people turn   the soil
of Rwanda   they find
its bones   they feel
its hearts'   my heart's
damage accumulate   damaged by
even gardens   accumulated pink
walks   even walks taken
pink orchids   (you would
think they would be
enough)   even Rwanda isn't
enough   an old symbol
metal and the flesh
blossoming rose   even the
gardens of Rwanda aren't
enough.

Ethnic cleansing

I don't want to be you or them.
They are the ones who come at night
  with or without hoods

  depending on
  which minister sends them

  depending on
  where you were born
  or where your parents were
  or where you are standing now.

We are the ones who let it happen
  again and again and again

and you are me sometimes
  and sometimes I am them.

The beach at Scheveningen

I watch Anne Frank
and her sister walk
towards the water   their
shoulder blades   sturdy legs
North Sea sandy goosebumps

Superman is somewhere else
He works through something
It grinds him down
'Must   resist   its   power'
WHAMMO!   A struggle between
yes and no   BLAM!
His dark determination pursues
the light   pushes at
otherwise immovable objects   KERPOW!
A comic book life
blasts into the contrastosphere

I have run away
from childhood   damp musty
smells   manual labour   to
a nice clean dry
loft   alone   a treehouse
no   a bunker   with
slits   a view of
the beach   watch against
invasion   back to the
dunes   work it out
that relief isn't coming
that running away isn't
an option   captured   hands
on head   led away

alive   Anne   me   Superman
turn   see limp gray
jellyfish come floating in

Snow fort in carport

Pausing in the carport by your snow fort, taken for granted year after year, I think about getting in.

As usual you've piled the snow around my metal-topped workbench, left it open at one end to make an entrance. Your shovel stands nearby.

When I parked, ice glittered in the fort: coloured blocks. We put food dye and water in yoghourt containers, left them out overnight.

Thawed, out slid your magic thoughts to be displayed on my chopping block: a wedge of wood; your altar; your stumpy kitchen table.

On all fours I bend my head, have to look at my knees to fit, feel fear rise in my throat.

It's cramped in here where the child still lives.

Boy

for David

'Piano lessons in your own home.' Me, desperate for money.
You sat at your kitchen table, eating Oreos with milk,
wanted to play Beethoven.
We struggled together as you grew from nine to twelve.
Didn't have the patience to learn how to learn. Just desire.
Your sister couldn't keep up. Keep up to you? Who could?
I barely recognized you at fifteen, pedalling your bike
breakneck down a hill,
and by the time I saw you again, it was only your name in the paper.
First of my students to predecease me.
I went to your wake that same night.
Listen: *Ode to Joy,* banged out, eighteen years' worth.
Your mother said 'We couldn't hold him.' Just hold him.
When you die young, the funeral parlour's full.

The old man leaves

Swimming goggles adjusted,
he steps into the shower,
stares out the small window.

In the front yard some of his things are piled for sale
and there's a homemade cardboard sign
on the inside dash of his car.

For the first time in fifty years
it's not pumpkins planted in the field
next to the house — but corn.

It was fun to see the orange appear out of green
and then jiggle them in the pick-up truck
to the IGA.

Out back he sits in a lawn chair,
eyelids down in the apple air,
hears no sound from the empty barns and sheds.

All those pigs and chickens,
he thinks.
Well, people have to eat.

At his check-up the doctor asks, any changes?
He replies, I'm losing my balance
but only when I close my eyes.

The old man drops

The old man feels the first pain grip,
thinks of the calves he helped birth,
pulls his SUV to the road's shoulder.
It's raining. Some cool air might be good.
Perhaps he shouldn't have cut and stacked that wood.

As the road is fast, he inches out the passenger door,
comes to the hood, leans first his palms
and then his brow on the cold wet metal,
remembers the feel of straining flesh.
The second contraction twists in his chest.

His hands clench, unclench, and with his head, rise
before he slides down the slippery side.

Back at his house, three woodpiles,
the opened hearts of trees.

The old man dreams

The old man looks
at a wooden kitchen chair — narrow —
with lean round legs.

He puts it on the fire escape
of his Montreal apartment
and dreams of 1950.

It's just for laughs

You know each woman makes her own pretence
though each pretence is similar,
and it's just for laughs inside the crystal ball:
the plumed nobleman on the plumed white charger.
So, when, outside the fortune-teller's tent, he swoops down,
woos her with flower and song — her face, her face — credulous,
incredulous,
then credulous again, as she mounts behind him,
only to discover the joke, and tears in my eyes,
to see how hard that dream dies.

Poor Barbie

Yup, she's still with us
Heels don't touch the ground
Can do the splits but nothing down there in between

Navel? Was she born at least
If she can't give birth? Nope

Big tits though
for man-hands
Nipples missing
Her desire missing
little hands

Poor Barbie, having a bad hair day?
You can see where the coronet was perched

Barbie, go away

A story told me

A story told me — pillow talk —
of a man beguiled by mother-love and mistress.

A man had such a wonderful mother
his mistress grew jealous of his love for her.
'Bring me,' she said, 'all of your mother's food.'

The man went to his mother's house and wept
and explained and his mother gave him all her food
and the man loved his mother very much.

But it was not enough for the jealous mistress.
'Bring me,' she cried, 'all of your mother's money.'
When the mother complied the man loved her more than ever.

His mistress grew tired of the man boasting about his mother.
'Bring me,' she screamed, 'your mother's heart.'
The man was silent. Then he visited his mother.

The mother listened to her son then opened her dress.
Her son put her dripping heart in a box but as he was leaving
her house he tripped on the doorsill.

From the box the mother's heart cried, 'God, break his fall.
My son is falling.' And the man went to his mistress' home
and murdered again.

Only the man left standing — beguiled by mother-love
and mistress — pillow talk.

Construction site

There is no way for a woman to comfortably pass.
It smells of the male; they root in its hole, bang things into place.

If she lowers her head, she is afraid.
If she raises it, she is proud.

If she looks away, she is coy.
If she looks hard, bold.

And she looks hard as a sweet young stud, sucking a cancer stick,
swings out of his pick-me-up truck, shoots her a glance.

#4 Mermaid Road

Seventy-five fit, scrawny years,
arms and legs tanned, sun-creased,
short white hair, glasses.
Wires support her teeth.

Encapsulated, she knows there is no 'ask me'
engraved on her forehead, no invitation.
Neither coquetry nor charm has ever
unwrinkled her brow's concentration.

Incompetent Venus, she looks to find the perfect shell.
Entire it shines: salt-washed, grit-free.
Gingerly she steps down on it,
foam drying in the breeze.

Mars

You might suppose I'm going to tell
of a planet lost, crisscrossed canals,
its glassy dust

Of cities found, of desert crust,
of fossil fern and date palms' must,
of bones that burn

I bring it down to one cheek, bare,
to one lip, soft, to softest hair,
beneath your sky

Water,
water once flowed there.

Woman, sitting

Somehow you have brought me beyond beauty.
You're scaring me now.
Can you not contain your hunger?
I can contain mine.
Look as it cracks open my chest, exposes my heart, spine.
Hunger is so very well contained by the frame of my life
that blood no longer drips around the edges, nor milk, nor tears.
I have become as dry as the Kalahari,
a place only a few consider beautiful.

Supermarket, Pie Neuf

We approach the cash.

The she-male, pushing six feet, has narrow hairy arms
and a flat bum, and is almost there.

Sh/he has a gentle face, sad and calm, and needs a two-inch dye-job
along her part to keep me guessing at her age.

But she is spending the money on sacks and cans of dog and cat food,
and kitty litter, instead.

'Without our pets, we'd be savages,' I pretend to say,
in my mind address her thin back, her spaghetti straps.

Beggar, Namur Station

The women come down the stairs
  like wet flowers

They watch their feet
  their heads bent like dripping flowers

He sits near the bottom of the escalator
  inhales the scent of moist flowers

As they come some raise their eyes
  and their lips prepare to curve like soft flowers

And they notice
  he is blind as a flower

Say you have an abortion

Say you have an abortion
say on a Wednesday
a sensible thing when you're poor and alone
and your kid might have been born
with your IUD stuck in its brain
and you're quite relieved
except for the bleeding
but on Sunday you don't really feel
like singing in church
so you walk your dog
and you lie on the sofa
listening to Brahms' *Requiem*
over and over
and though it's spring
the grass is a little less green
than it was last Tuesday
and you practise being old.

The garden

How shall I describe the garden?
I shall describe it thus:
secret, shady, beautiful, mysterious.
Like us.

How shall I conserve the garden?
I shall conserve it hence:
as a temporary, cool, sweet oasis.
No fence.

And how shall I kill the garden?
Because it has to die.
Sow bitter herbs beneath a salty flood.
And lie.

Iynx

When I'm dying will I finally hold myself tenderly?
Yes, yes, tears and mother-death.
The last view blots out the busy life before.

My lover's mother took his hair and nail clippings
so no one else could jinx him, burned them in her water pipe.
First son. First live son. Ishmael. The sun.

I say the incantation.
On a loop of string a small wheel hums as it unwinds.
Twisting my neck from side to side,

I use nymph's potion,
made from birds whose necks were wrung,
to pull him near me.

Temporary Iynx, I have him.
She fakes a heart attack.
He's gone, mother-won.

Note: Iynx (pronounced Yunx) was a Greek nymph in charge of love potions who was turned by a vengeful goddess into a bird (a wryneck, genus Jynx) that, when threatened, can turn its neck almost completely around.

on the death of one

crying the midwife held him
smiling because his spirit was there
  and it was bright
smiling and crying she held him

but he was already gone
  and begun cooling
  and the rules requested his body

slowly we processed from the room
  to the nurses' station
you held him like a precious offering
we were silent as we gave him up

it was a mysterious death
clearly the autopsy, the autopsy
  answered none of my questions

there was a woman with tissues
  at the funeral home
there were forms to fill out
I wrote a cheque for fifty dollars

there was paperwork also at the cemetery
an old man there promised he would bury him himself
this was all he could offer

I imagined a small box or a sack
I imagined there would have to be plastic
  as later I visited that earth

fresh dug at the side of the road
  where the buried unborn stretched small hands
  to catch me passing

the old man had scattered straw
  and I saw I had entered a new land
  with old, old customs

Word music

For two readers reading line by line or simultaneously or alternating stanzas or columns; in whatever direction they wish.

I wish
I had
a robe
of white

White hood
pulled up
to warm
my head

my cheeks
my jaw
my ach-
ing tongue.

to cloak
my sore
mistak-
en tongue.

I wish
I do
soft snow
might fall

Instead
I know
sharp snow
will fall

to cov
er me
in ut-
ter sleep.

and coz-
en me
to ut-
ter sleep.

Lilac, lilac

In the new light made by the cutting down
I count the rings in the lilac stumps.
Each stump has a lilac stain halfway —
between heartwood, and bark.

Twenty years since love was so strong
it planted fragrance near the bedroom window,
planted too close for the house's health:
roots pierce the foundation.

And yes, I would smell lilac every spring.
And yes, I would think of the planter.
And suddenly I'm crying, laughing,
singing 'lilac, lilac' as I cut them down.

Guitar lessons: a cowgirl poem

Rebuilding the left hand after thirty years — tough,
when every barre chord screams of you,
short nails left, long right, still revolt
and steel's slid squeaks evoke
bruised then calloused fingertips.

Looking to get back on one horse that threw me.
Would you have me dust off that ancient saddle,
tighten its girth and sing?

Swallowed remembrances grip at throat strings.
Tears ride me away.

I am silent about God

I am silent about God
because I know what he wants.

Like all abusers
he wants me to love him anyway.

Sorry, God, I whisper,
you can't have it both ways.

My eye pressed up to your eye,
tooth hooked onto tooth.

Feathers

How good for the coyote
to feel their softness
blunt-tipped

with teeth marks at one quill's thick end
the way you chew a pen.
A little blood

a white blotch where the bird —
no time to clean —
the equivalent accident

a bus and dirty underpants.
These words
(traps that I fall into)

so easy to drop —
the soft feathers at my feet —
only feathers.

Something dropped them
something fell
and when I let go your hand

I fall out of the world.
Tell me where to go.

abstract

how
paint this page
with words so pale
it still looks white
when finished

should
thin meaning
sameness
a light technique
spare

or blacken it
with murder
tar?

I am not a man

When I sense danger, I turn to it.
  Want to go berserk.

Morbid humour suits me: I laugh
  as I swing my axe at the clay-born.

They gurgle as they sink back.
  Their castle walls whisper wetly.

When I am cut, sparks fly up,
  as my light kindles.

As I run stiffly towards him,
  Death grins in my face

and I stop, grin back, and roar:
  I am not a man. *I am a Viking.*

29 words on solitude

Sometimes chosen, often not.

    Society can tell.

I've got emotional leprosy.

    Bits of me are dropping off.

Not so bad. When I walk out,

    I can hear my bell.

11:23 a.m.

I'm in some pain today
but the pain gives a nice edge
to the clouds in the sky
and I never played the piano
as well as that six months
I suffered the toothache.
Six months till the dentist, bless her,
gave up and pulled the noisy bastard.
Now I tickle its ghost place
when I want to concentrate.
That was the summer I understood
why the old and the ill enjoy a few drinks.
'You can keep your anti-inflammatories.
Enflame me with whatever you're pouring.'
Alcohol, applied directly to the nerve.

Winter

In the white dress I stand in the white room.

There's a blue icicle light.

The blue icicle light lets me see

the pleasing white bones of my face.

The pleasing white bones and muscles smile:

hello (and) goodbye.

I manage my mask. The wrinkles hurt —

but not enough to cry.

My new face

The woman asks everyone she meets:
did you bring me my new face?
Did you bring me one with a bright
curved beak? Or one with melting bones?
She cries: my new face.

And she loves you the way fire loves a forest.

Most terrifying is her effect indoors.
Everything electrical smoulders:
every lamp, every appliance.
Every wire hidden in the wall
burns through the plaster, must be smothered.

Twice this year and twice last year

Tax returns to a low earner equal entitlements.
More if there are children.

Legislation plus four new winter tires lead to
surprise! Manufacturer's rebate.

Miscellaneous occupations for bottom feeders
in any large city's ads: focus groups, small brief jobs at weddings and
funerals: anything that pays cash.

Afraid to answer the one that reappears with alarming regularity:
cage cleaner for reptile collection.

WWJD

(with a nod to Nash)

What would Jesus do
if he were alive?
What would Jesus do?
How many times would he die?

Would he be that jungle priest?
Would he sit down with the beast
at an international conference?

What would Jesus do
if he sat down next to you?
What would he find to say?

Would he talk of silk pajamas,
parachutes or Dalai lamas;
would he ask you if you knew
one hell or two?

Tell me 'cause I need to know:
would you pray
for him to stay
or go?

Reading Neruda, 2009

This man sucked in all available words;
combined them in all possible phrases.
If I use the word born he is there.
If I use the word blood he is there.
And so with fern, land, woman bread, brother man —
what I have already written is informed by him
even though I am only now reading him
for the first time, in my fifty-second year.

She set the woods on fire

She set the woods on fire
with a few stray words
she'd thought were out
when she dumped them on the ash pile
but some were still glowing
and the tip of a raspberry cane,
bent by snow, caught their heat,
passed it to the broken birch at the edge,
through maple and beech,
to the heart of the woods,
even into the oak,
whose hearts would burn a hundred years.

Stolen

While I was at the library today
the poetry thief was busy. When I
got home I found all my poems out of
their files loose and mixed-up on the floor. Death
poems lay with love poems. Nature po-
ems covered the political ones. Con-
fessional and narrative had become
confused. When viewed from above, experi-
mental and formalist styles appeared sim-
ilar. And when I started to sort through
and re-file all the poems, I discov-
ered that the ones about sex and drugs and
liquor were gone. So I knew the poet-
ry thief was just some kid passing the time.

Rest

Night the keeper of mysteries and of
understandings its work leaves you
sore waking exhausted only day-sleep so
shallow seems uncomplicated an escape
from the seven things you do before
lunch the thirteen before supper
you list them on your fingers as you fall asleep
they seemed necessary at the time
to use the body or lose it the mind
the same the work for house garden
money needs to come in go out
purposeful breathing involuntary

Angel, linocut on linen

Angel, feet in lilies, eagle wings.
One hand holds one lily, trimmed.
Red hair ripples, floats.

She gazes, steady,
from a star, sun, moon-filled sky,
offers you tranquility, direct.

Tick tick tick. She fills the page.
The lily drips.

Six lines

Some still love a beautiful thing:
the weight of a stone in the hand;
a looking down, a looking up;
I promise you this is the place
where we gaze at the sun but have no need to fly near it.

Throw the stone. Again. Again.

One morning

You shake with wonder
the bamboo palm shivers by the open window
its shadow trembles on the sofa cushion
light and air and sound smooth together

There is a moment after sleep when you can't
quite believe it's all there to do over
the buses you caught the line-ups the other faces
turned inward may have been dream splinters

The small hearts zipped in your jacket keep you warm
you are unsure are you a street-person
who keeps pets and begs for their food
creatures together

You know by now there is no application
no form to fill out that can keep you
from being you except there will be one
one morning

Others will have to bother you'll be
running the clover soft rain fills your footprints
you release the clocks and they go up
into the trees singing

Long ago

and far away
a woman trudged
with head bent into the storm
for of course snow was falling
and a cruel wind pressed it
into her face…

long ago and far away
she felt silk slip to the floor
the oriental purple and gold pattern
she would know in her dreams
and there was only surprise
at the identity of the embracer
when she awoke and then very little
surprise really only that there should
be more than one…

night followed night
and they embraced her one after the other
all the refusals, all the denials,
even, a few, laughing,
and she thought, there,
that's taken care of that,
how easy, how pleasant, how relieved I am
to have finished acting.

Grace

I was asleep a minute ago.
I was asleep, I was

then something jangled — music,
a man's voice

and I had to come back, to rise,
to wash, lay down the day's load

in a different place, again try
to find sweet oblivion — untaxed,

absolutely serene. // Absolute serenity
as when the food and water come,

the people, kind people, are there
and the little house touches you

as you sit, lie down, as you
stand, stretch your arms, its walls

are there, they are wood and stone,
its roof is there, right there, and out

the window, some glass, some natural sound
clear and certain. // At first

you are afraid. There is no way
to lock the door. The little house

trembles in the wood at night.
The narrow bed imagines itself underground

but the walls sparkle. They
hold jewels meant to catch star or moon

radiance. // Radiant life returns with
dawn. You hear the people pass.

Their soft murmurs persuade you back
to sleep. You know what you have to do

and you do it. // So many ways
to be amazed, fife and cymbal,

a body's slick undulation, dozens
of shadflies, rising up from leaf mould

after the first frost. Woken by sun,
they call then settle again.

Brief, mad day, worth anything.

About the Author

Born in Montreal and raised in Hudson, Quebec, Louise Carson studied music in Montreal and Toronto, played jazz piano and sang in the chorus of the Canadian Opera Company. While *A Clearing* is her first full-length collection of poetry, Carson has contributed to numerous chapbooks and her poems have been published in literary magazines from coast to coast as well as in *The Best Canadian Poetry 2013*. She's twice been short-listed in *FreeFall Magazine*'s annual contest, and her poem "Plastic bucket" won a Manitoba Magazine Award for *Prairie Fire*. She currently lives in rural Quebec, where she gardens, writes, and teaches music.

Eco-Audit
Printing this book using Rolland Opaque 30 instead of virgin fibres paper saved the following resources:

Solid Waste	Water	Air Emissions
19 kg	1,536 L	172 kg